Undertaking a foster carer review

A guide to collecting and analysing information for a foster carer review using Form FR (England)

Paul Adams

BAAF
ADOPTION & FOSTERING
www.baaf.org.uk

Published by
British Association for Adoption & Fostering
(BAAF)
Saffron House
6–10 Kirby Street
London EC1N 8TS
www.baaf.org.uk

Charity registration 275689 (England and Wales) and SC039337 (Scotland)

British Library Cataloguing in Publication Data
A catalogue record for this book is available from the British Library

ISBN 978 1 910039 18 2

Project management by Jo Francis, Publications, BAAF
Designed and typeset by Helen Joubert Designs
Printed in Great Britain by The Lavenham Press

BAAF is the leading UK-wide membership organisation for all those concerned
with adoption, fostering and child care issues.

Contents

Acknowledgements

Work on BAAF Form FR has been ongoing for some time and discussions about review formats generally were undertaken initially with a group of practitioners, including Jane Davis (Hull City Council), Caron Gill (East Riding Council), and Joan Hunt (BAAF). It was following these discussions that Form FR was developed.

The forms were trialled by a small pilot group consisting of both local authority and independent fostering services: Doncaster Metropolitan Borough Council (Kevan Shaw), Kasper Fostering (Amy Ansell), Leeds City Council (Val Hales), London Borough of Wandsworth (David Brooks), Orange Grove Fostercare (John Heron), and Team Fostering (Kathleen Walley). This exercise led to a number of changes and further developments.

BAAF is very grateful to all of these individuals for their contributions, to Alexandra Conroy Harris (BAAF) for legal consultation, and to Florence Merredew and her colleagues on the BAAF Health Group Advisory Committee for their input to the section on foster carers and their health. Thanks also go to Elaine Dibben and Joan Hunt at BAAF, and Sarah Bevan (independent social worker) for their comments on the original draft. Shaila Shah and Jo Francis have offered helpful advice and turned a manuscript into the finished article.

On many issues there have been different views and perspectives expressed, and often there has been no consensus; the only person who can be held responsible for any identified shortcomings in the final product is the author.

Note
This guide has been kindly supported by funding from the Esmée Fairbairn Foundation.

The author

Paul Adams qualified as a social worker in 1993, having been inspired by working as a foster carer in the US. He has worked predominantly in local authority children's services, managing child care and fostering teams.

Paul joined BAAF as a Fostering Development Consultant in 2010. He has written Good Practice Guides on parent and child fostering, contact in permanent placements, social work with Gypsy, Roma and Traveller children, and dogs and other pets in fostering and adoption. Paul has also developed BAAF Form C (connected persons), BAAF Form FR (foster carer reviews) and considerably revised BAAF Form F (fostering assessments) in England. He is an experienced Chair of fostering and adoption panels, and an adopter.

Paul lives in North Wales with his partner Sarah, daughters Louisha and Sherissa, and rescue dogs Simba and Bluebell.

Introduction

It is fundamental that supervising social workers and others working in fostering services understand the significance of the foster carer review process. This is clearly and helpfully set out by Cosis Brown (2011, p 86):

> *Foster carer reviews are central building blocks to monitoring and improving the quality of foster care and in so doing the quality of experience for foster children. They are important. Some would argue that they are more important than the foster carer assessment as it is through the foster carer review process that evidence is presented about the actual rather than the hypothetical quality of fostering that a foster carer has undertaken.*

Foster carer reviews, if done rigorously and analytically, establish whether or not a foster carer and their household remain suitable to care for foster children and if their terms of approval remain appropriate. This in itself is crucial for safeguarding foster children's well-being, as described in detail by Biehall *et al* (2014).

As well as being a central safeguarding mechanism, reviews offer the opportunity to focus on the development of a foster carer and how a fostering service can facilitate that foster carer's work as well as their development. Reviews offer the possibility through the evaluation of a foster carer's fostering practice to praise them for the good work undertaken and the considerable contribution that they make to a foster child's life, their family and to the wider community.

As the term indicates, the review process constitutes a review of the period since the last review (often a year), bringing together all that has happened in that period, and results in a report that provides significant evidence about the foster carer's current strengths, abilities and areas for development. The review report is an important and significant document, and this good practice guide offers advice in relation to each of the different contributions that make up the review report.

In practice, we know that fostering services have some very different ideas about what a review process should look like. For those fostering services achieving the highest standards, the importance of the process is well understood and considerable time and effort is invested in making this a meaningful exercise. For others, the review is not given the attention that it warrants (Pearlman, 2012; Ingham, 2013) and is completed quickly and superficially in order to comply with the legal requirements.

BAAF's Form FR (England) is a set of forms that are intended very much for the former, with a view to encouraging careful analysis, discussion and reflection. The expectations that come with using Form FR are high, but not unrealistic, and this standard of practice is routinely achieved by a number of local authorities and independent fostering providers.

It is important to be clear about the purpose of the foster carer review, which is primarily about whether a foster carer and their household remain suitable to foster, and whether the terms of approval continue to be appropriate. There is an assumption that the foster carers were suitable at the time of approval, and the first, and subsequent reviews are designed to consider whether that remains the case. Whereas the assessment has considered someone's potential to foster, the review process considers the reality of what that means.

So, a review is not a reassessment of suitability, although conducting a review effectively will of course require some of the skills that are used in undertaking an assessment; and the social worker and reviewing officer will need to keep an open mind if evidence emerges to suggest that earlier judgements about suitability were flawed. Although the review is expected primarily to consider the review period, it is necessary to consider this in the context of everything that is known about the foster carer and their household, and to take account of historical information.

The chapters that follow provide some general information about legal and other frameworks under which reviews take place, and consider the planning of reviews with suggested timescales for each part of the process. A lengthy chapter then provides detailed guidance about the use of each individual report within Form FR, before looking at achieving the Training, Support and Development Standards (TSDS). Subsequent chapters give consideration to reviewing the foster carer's health and looking at the policies that are relevant in undertaking a review. The final chapter brings the issues together in a short conclusion.

Terminology

Within this guide, the term "fostering service provider" or "fostering service" is used to cover both local authority fostering services and independent fostering providers (IFPs). It discusses foster carer reviews, although equally might use the term foster home review.

While in practice different terms are used to describe fostering social workers, this guide prefers the term "supervising social worker", as this is the term used in the statutory guidance definitions and throughout the National Minimum Standards. The term "supervising social worker" also accurately describes what that role should be.

The term "reviewing officer" is used to describe the person who chairs the review meeting, assuming that such a meeting takes place and that the Chair is not also the allocated supervising social worker. It should be noted that although the structure of some fostering services does not provide for a reviewing officer, this role is deemed necessary to achieve good practice (UK Joint Working Party on Foster Care, 1999) and this guidance does not therefore address circumstances where no such post or process exists.

Sons and daughters of foster carers are mentioned in the text, and readers will need to use their judgement to take account of children on other legal orders such as special guardianship where, for all intents and purposes, they are in the same position as birth or adopted children. The term "foster carer" is used in the singular, but equally applies to couples who are fostering together.

Before using Form FR

This guide has been specifically written to assist fostering services that are using Form FR as the tool for conducting foster carer reviews. It is not normally permissible for BAAF forms licence holders to amend the forms for their own use without having specific written permission, but in relation to Form FR, BAAF is agreeable to relatively minor amendments to meet local requirements. This is because the regulations and guidance in relation to foster home reviews allow for considerable flexibility, and practice across fostering services is very varied. In practice, this means that fostering services may choose to remove any sections from the forms, or make *minor* wording changes to reflect local arrangements.

In a number of places in Form FR-A, the registered manager of the fostering service is invited to 'detail the policy requirements of your fostering service' in order to maximise the flexibility and usefulness of the forms. It is expected that the registered manager (or, with their express permission, someone appropriate within the service) should make these insertions and save them to the forms, before circulating them to practitioners within the fostering service. The registered manager is also permitted to replace the word "name" with "initials" in the forms wherever appropriate, and in line with that fostering service's policy.

Any such changes should be undertaken only after careful consideration of the legal requirements in relation to foster home reviews, and subject to a prominent note being clearly added to the form, that states:

> *This form has been amended by [name of fostering service] from the original BAAF version, and BAAF cannot be held responsible for any shortcomings or limitations arising from these amendments.*

It is not permissible to add additional sections *within* the individual FR forms, although there is nothing to stop fostering services adding an entirely separate additional form or forms. Any additional forms should not carry the BAAF logo, and should be labelled as '[Name of agency] additional form for use with BAAF Form FR (England)'.

Fostering services may also wish to use a form of their own to replace any one or more of the individual forms in Form FR. This is permissible, again on the proviso that the alternative form does not carry the BAAF logo, and has a clear heading that distinguishes it from Form FR.

Limitations of Form FR and this guide

Form FR was not designed with kinship foster carers or short break foster carers specifically in mind, although there is nothing within the forms that prevents them from being used with either of these groups of carers. Although the Training, Support and Development Standards (TSDS) that are identified within the forms correlate to mainstream fostering, Form FR has been used with these groups on occasions within the pilot, and experience suggests that, if used flexibly, it can be an effective and appropriate tool for this purpose.

Individual fostering services will need to make their own decisions about how best to review kinship and short break foster carers according to their own preferences and the local situation. Unless there are indications of a demand for this, BAAF does not intend to produce review forms specific to these particular groups of foster carers.

It should also be acknowledged that this guide does not consider the IRM process (in England and Wales), since although this is important, it is separate from the actual foster carer review process. Nevertheless, it is worth noting that where a fostering service has undertaken a high quality review, this will reflect well on them, and the information contained within the papers will be helpful if the case ultimately reaches the IRM.

The legal framework

Fostering Services (England) Regulations (2011)

The legal framework for fostering reviews is set out in Regulation 28 of the Fostering Services (England) Regulations (2011) and states that the fostering service must:

> ... *review the approval of each foster carer not more than a year after approval (and after that whenever necessary, but at intervals not exceeding a year) in order to consider whether the foster carer and their household continues to be suitable.*

In undertaking the review, regulations state that the fostering service must:

- seek and take into account the views of the foster carer;

- seek and take into account the views of any child placed with the foster carer (subject to age and understanding);

- seek and take into account the views of any placing authority which has, within the preceding year, placed a child with the foster carer (in practice this means the views of the child's social worker);

- make such enquiries and obtain such information as they consider necessary.

At the conclusion of the review, the fostering service provider must prepare a written report that sets out whether the foster carer and their household continue to be suitable, and whether their terms of approval continue to be suitable. It is important to be clear about when the review is complete. In most circumstances this will be following the entire review process and when the fostering service has produced their written report, usually signed off by a fostering manager.

The first review after approval must be presented to the fostering panel, and any subsequent reviews may be presented to the fostering panel at the discretion of the fostering service.

If, after a review and taking into account any fostering panel recommendations, the fostering service decision-maker considers that a foster carer continues to be suitable, with their terms unchanged, then the fostering service provider is required to inform the foster carer of this in writing. There is also a specified process to follow if it is decided that the foster carer is no longer suitable, or if it is decided that their terms of approval need to be changed.

The statutory guidance that accompanies the regulations adds very little, other than to clarify that seeking the views of the placing authority in effect means contacting the social worker for any child who has been placed.

Fostering Services National Minimum Standards (2011)

Similarly, the Fostering Services National Minimum Standards (2011) are largely silent in terms of how foster carer reviews should be undertaken, save for requiring that:

> *Reviews of foster carers' approval are sufficiently thorough to allow the fostering service to properly satisfy itself about their carers' ongoing suitability to foster.* (NMS 13.8)

While this might be interpreted as requiring a detailed and comprehensive process, the requirement is vague, meaning that in practice there is significant variation across fostering services in relation to how reviews are completed, and the formats that are used for this purpose. Depending on how NMS 13.8 is viewed, it may be possible to comply with regulatory requirements without achieving what many others might deem to be good practice. In this context, it is worth looking at another helpful framework.

UK National Standards for Foster Care (1999)

Although the UK National Standards for Foster Care (UK Joint Working Party on Foster Care, 1999) have never been legally binding, the standards that they set for foster care reviews are helpful in giving an idea about what good practice might look like. Until the revisions in 2011, the introduction to the Fostering Services Regulations and National Minimum Standards 2002 indicated that the UK National Standards 'represent best practice and as such should be fully complied with by fostering service providers'. These are set out in full in this good practice guide (see box below), and the following key aspects have been accepted as best practice and incorporated into the process using Form FR:

- there is an agreed format for the review which includes the carer's views on the support that they receive;

- the review format includes:
  - updates of any required checks
  - the views of parents where appropriate
  - the views of sons and daughters
  - the views of other household members
  - the foster carer's training and support needs going forward;

- a review meeting involving the foster carer and supervising social worker is chaired by an appropriate independent third party.

UK National Standards for Foster Care (1999)

There is an agreed format for the foster carer review which incorporates both the assessed performance of the carer and the carer's assessment of the quality of service and support provided by the authority, as well as any required updates of statutory checks.

- A review report is compiled by the supervising social worker, incorporating the written views of each social worker responsible for any child placed in the foster home since the last review, the views of the children who are fostered and their parents where appropriate, and the views of the carer, her or his sons and daughters and any other household members.

- The review report includes an action plan for the next 12 months, identified training and support needs of the carer and a recommendation regarding continued approval of the carer, and the numbers and ages of children for whom she or he is approved.

- The carer has the opportunity to read the review report and to contribute her or his own written comments.

- The review includes repeats of all statutory checks and references for the carer at least once every three years.

- A review meeting is held that includes the carer and the supervising social worker, and is chaired by an appropriate third party, who can form an independent judgement and is knowledgeable about foster care.

- Where necessary, the carer is supported to play a full part in the review through provision of disabled access, translation and interpreting facilities.

- Each annual review of a carer requires the endorsement of the fostering panel; where there is any change in the circumstances of the carer, or the outcome of the review is a recommendation for change or termination of approval, a recommendation or decision is reached by the panel and the carer has the right to put her or his view to the panel meeting.

- The carer receives written notification of the outcome of the review and the reasons for it, together with details of any appeal or complaints procedure.

- The report of the review meeting and its outcome are recorded on the carer's file, together with any relevant comments or objections from the carer.

- An additional review is held following any significant incidents, complaints or allegations of abuse or neglect.

Terms of approval

Central to the undertaking of foster carer reviews is a proper understanding of the legal requirements around setting terms of approval, and recognition of the need to do this.

Regulation 25(1)(b) states that, where the fostering panel makes a recommendation about a person's suitability to foster, its function is also 'to recommend any terms on which the approval is to be given'. Guidance clarifies that this might be in terms of the number of children and their ages. Regulation 25(2)(a) states that the panel 'must take into account all the information passed to it', so if that information suggests to the panel that a foster carer is suitable for a particular number of children, or children of a particular age range, then it must make a recommendation accordingly.

This means that at the time of the first review the foster carers will usually have terms of approval based on numbers and age of children, unless of course they have been specifically deemed suitable to foster a range of children and no terms are set. If foster carers are approved as suitable to foster three children aged 0–18, this *does* constitute the setting of terms. Regulation 28(4) requires the fostering service to consider whether terms continue to be appropriate, and to change them if necessary.

Frequently asked questions

What checks and references need to be updated as part of the foster carer review process?

There is no legal requirement to update any checks or references, although fostering services may have their own policies in regards to this matter. Since it is now possible and relatively straightforward for fostering services to complete online Disclosure and Barring Service (DBS) checks, there are strong arguments for updating these as part of all foster carer reviews.

Is the foster carer review complete when the review meeting is held, or when the decision-maker makes the decision?

Neither. The review process is complete when the fostering service has compiled their report and made a recommendation regarding the foster carer's continued suitability. Using Form FR, this is when Form FR-H has been completed by the fostering service manager.

When must a foster carer review be presented to the panel?

A foster carer review must be presented to the panel where this is the first review after approval. Fostering service policies may require that panels consider reviews in other circumstances, such as routinely every three years or when considering termination of approval or a change in terms of approval, or following allegations or a complaint.

If relevant new information comes to light after the review is completed, but before the decision is made, can the decision-maker take account of this?

In these circumstances, consideration of this "new" information can be seen as part of the same review process. Foster carers should be made aware of the information (unless there is reason not to do this) and be given an opportunity to respond in writing, and the fostering manager should resubmit a concluding report. The decision-maker can then make their decision.

Is it possible to change terms of approval without holding a foster carer review?

No. A foster carer review is the only way to change terms of approval. However, it is possible to arrange for a temporary placement outside of terms of approval for a maximum of six working days.

3

The foster carer review process

Planning the review

The foster carer review process needs to be administered efficiently, with careful consideration of timescales, and with systems in place to check on responses and follow up if they are not forthcoming. In some cases, this activity will be undertaken by dedicated administrative staff, sometimes by the supervising social worker, and sometimes by the two working closely together. Where administrators are involved in the process this can be of great benefit, but it is important that their role does not stray into that which is more properly the responsibility of the supervising social worker. For example, while it is entirely appropriate for an administrator to chase up missing responses from children's social workers, it would not be appropriate for them to record the social worker's views based on a telephone conversation, as this is effectively a casework discussion that should be had first-hand by the supervising social worker.

Each fostering service will need to have a policy and procedure regarding the administration of the foster carer review, and the advice in this chapter may be helpful in formulating this. The planning flowcharts (and the discussion within the following paragraphs) offer one set of proposed timescales and activities, but there is no legal compunction to follow this approach; other arrangements may be equally valid.

Before the review meeting

The review process should start about six weeks before the review meeting with Forms FR-B, FR-C, FR-D, FR-E, and FR-F being circulated to the appropriate parties for completion and return. A system will need to be in place to monitor progress and to chase up any outstanding returns. The supervising social worker will also need to start work on their report using Form FR-A.

Arrangements should also be put in place to update any checks or references, depending on the requirements of the fostering service policy. If fostering service policy requires checks or foster carer medicals to be updated periodically, then because of the time that this might take, there may need to be a specific system in place that does not rely on the annual review process. The review process will then serve as a further check that nothing has been missed.

By about four weeks before the review meeting, the supervising social worker should have completed the first draft of their Form FR-A. This, with completed Forms FR-B, FR-C, FR-D, FR-E, and FR-F, should then be passed to the fostering manager for consideration and comment. The fostering manager then has the opportunity to look at the papers that will be available to the review meeting, and to quality-assure the supervising social worker report. It is important that the manager looks at these papers at the earliest opportunity, as if changes to Form FR-A are needed, for example, possibly after further conversations with the foster carer, then there will need to be time for this activity to take place.

Where changes are suggested, it may be that the fostering manager asks to see the papers again, but with or without that, the whole set of completed papers (FR-A, FR-B, FR-C, FR-D, FR-E, and FR-F) should be circulated to the foster carer and the reviewing officer two weeks in advance of the review meeting. If the content of the papers includes information or views that the foster carer is unaware of, or if there is significant criticism of the carer, good practice would dictate that the supervising social worker considers the best way to share the papers, most likely taking them in person and discussing their contents. The two-week period prior to the meeting will allow the reviewing officer to seek any clarifications in advance of the meeting where necessary, and will also allow the foster carer to consider and reflect on any comments about their practice.

The review meeting

The dates for the review meeting should be set a long way in advance, and reviews are required to be completed within 12 months of approval, and at subsequent intervals not exceeding 12 months. However, because the review is only completed when the fostering manager has signed it off using Form FR-H, it is important that in setting review dates the practitioners take account of the fact that there is some activity required after the actual review meeting, that must also fall within this 12-month timescale.

It is therefore recommended that the first review is scheduled for 11 months after the date of approval, as this will ensure that there is sufficient time for review minutes to be completed and for the fostering manager to finalise the review process. This recommendation is based on an expectation that the reviewing officer has two weeks to write up the report following the meeting, and that the fostering manager has a further two weeks to finalise the process. This total of four weeks should be sufficient to take account of other demands and issues including annual leave and the like.

When considering subsequent review dates after the first review, there are two options. The most straightforward option is for the reviewing officer, at the end of each review meeting, to set a date for the following review meeting, and to make that 11 months later. This will meet the requirement of completing reviews at intervals not exceeding 12 months.

Alternatively, someone in the fostering service could keep track of the actual date on which the review was completed (that is, when the fostering manager completed Form FR-H) and set the subsequent review meeting 11 months after that date. This has the disadvantage that the next review meeting cannot be set at the conclusion of the previous review meeting, and requires a separate administrative process for setting these dates. However, the advantage is that the interval between reviews would potentially be longer (by between 1–27 days), while still remaining within the 12 month requirement.

After the review meeting

On completion of the review meeting, it is anticipated that the reviewing officer will write their report, using Form FR-G, within two weeks. Where the issues are contentious or disputed, best practice is for the reviewing officer to share their report with the foster carer and offer the opportunity for a written response. The completed forms (FR-A to FR-G, and any response from the foster carer) will then be passed to the fostering manager for consideration and so that he or she can complete Form FR-H within a further two weeks. This constitutes the end of the fostering review, and the date that the review is completed is the date entered by the fostering manager on Form FR-H.

While a total of four weeks is envisaged for the activity that follows the review meeting, it is desirable that this is completed more quickly where possible, so that a decision can be reached about suitability, and the foster carer notified. Particularly where cases are going to be presented at a fostering panel, it is helpful to avoid delay, so that the information being presented is as up to date as possible. It is also hoped that reviewing officers and managers will be mindful of panel dates so that any deadlines for the submission of papers can be met wherever possible.

After the foster carer review

Upon completion of the review, the fostering manager will need to pass the full set of papers to either the fostering panel administrator if the case is going to be heard at the panel, or directly to the decision-maker. If the case has been considered by the panel, then minutes for that item should be attached to the review papers and passed to the decision-maker. In either event, from the receipt of the papers, the decision-maker has seven working days to decide about the foster carer's continued approval on the same terms, or to make a qualifying determination if they are minded to terminate or vary the terms, and to notify the fostering manager by completing Form FR-I. Within seven working days of having received that decision or qualifying determination, the fostering manager must ensure that written notification has been provided to the foster carer.

Pre-foster carer review planning flowchart	
Six weeks before the review meeting	Circulate Forms FR-B, FR-C, FR-D, FR-E, and FR-F for completion and return. Update checks in line with fostering service policy. Begin work on Form FR-A.
Four weeks before the review meeting	Pass completed Forms FR-A (draft), FR-B, FR-C, FR-D, FR-E, and FR-F to fostering manager.
Two weeks before the review meeting	Finalise Form FR-A (taking into account any comments from the fostering manager). Circulate all completed forms (FR-A to FR-F) to the foster carer and reviewing officer.
Review meeting	
Within two weeks of the review meeting	Complete Form FR-G (reviewing officer) and pass all forms (FR-A to FR-G) to the fostering manager. (Where there is conflict and disagreement, the reviewing officer should offer the foster carer an opportunity to see their report and submit written comments.)
Within four weeks of the review meeting	Complete Form FR-H (fostering manager) to complete the review process.

Post-foster carer review planning flowchart	
Upon completion of the review	Pass completed forms (FR-A to FR-H) to either the panel administrator or the decision-maker.
Where applicable	The fostering panel considers the case and makes a recommendation regarding continued suitability of the foster carers. Pass completed forms (FR-A to FR-H) and panel minutes to the decision-maker.
Within seven working days of having received papers	The decision-maker decides on continued suitability and completes Form FR-I. He or she passes Form FR-I back to the fostering manager.
Within seven working days of having received the decision	Foster carers are provided with written notice of the decision or qualifying determination.

Undertaking a review at short notice

The information above sets out best practice in undertaking a foster carer review, and assumes that there is time for careful planning. Since most reviews are undertaken annually this is usually the case, but there is one notable exception – when a review is necessary within six working days to allow for a child placed temporarily outside of approval terms to lawfully remain in a particular foster home. Although a review conducted in these circumstances must comply with all legal requirements – there is no such thing as a "brief review" or "interim review" – in practice it will of course be more challenging to complete the process to the same quality as might normally be the case.

In this scenario, the supervising social worker and their manager will need to ensure that time is prioritised to undertake this work, and this will include preparing a sufficiently detailed supervising social worker report, obtaining a foster carer report, and making time to meaningfully seek the views of the children in the foster home. It will also be necessary to obtain a report from the social worker for any child in placement. It may be that it is not possible to seek the views of others, but wherever possible, this would be helpful. It may be that a quick telephone call or email exchange is the most that can be realistically achieved.

If a review has been conducted relatively recently, it might be appropriate to make use of paperwork that has been completed previously, although it is important wherever possible to check that the information contained within this review remains accurate and reflects the views of the person who completed it.

The reviewing officer for a review convened at short notice will need to strike a balance between accepting that the paperwork may not be at the usual high standard, yet also requiring enough information to be able to make a confident recommendation about widening terms of approval. It should be remembered that there was probably a good reason why the narrower approval terms were agreed at the previous review, and in looking at cases of abuse or neglect in care, Biehal *et al* noted that there were 'some examples of carers being approved to foster more children than they previously had – sometimes at their own request – and then struggling to cope' (2014, p 101). The needs of the placing service should not unduly influence thinking about what is realistic and in the best interests of any children placed.

Where a review has been conducted at short notice, and information is more limited than might normally be the case, it might be appropriate for any terms of approval to be limited to named specific children. It might also be appropriate for the review date that was set at the previous review to remain in place, rather than to wait another 11 months from the review that was set at short notice. These are all matters that should be addressed in the relevant fostering service policy.

Using Form FR

4

Form FR-A: Supervising social worker report

Form FR-A, the supervising social worker report, should be the most comprehensive report in the set of reports that make up Form FR. It should provide detailed evidence about the foster carers and their household, and offer a picture of their fostering experience over the period since the previous review – usually a year. While this is expected to be a significant piece of work, it should not require the supervising social worker to gather any new information, but to present what is known from having worked with the foster carers throughout that period. The review should be an integral part of an ongoing process that reflects the relationship between the foster carer and the fostering service in the person of the supervising social worker. The content of the report should not therefore offer any surprises to the foster carer, as any matters of concern should have already been discussed with them in the context of the supervisory relationship.

Before becoming available to the supervising social worker, the blank copy of Form FR-A should have been edited by the registered manager (or someone to whom they delegated the task) so that it contains the relevant policy and other information specific to the fostering service in which it is being used (see Chapter 1). In some fostering services, an administrator is involved in completing the factual parts of the form where that requires checking historical dates and entering information about dates when checks and the like were completed. In such situations, it is important that this does not stray into social work activity, and the supervising social worker must be aware that they are signing off the report, and so need to be satisfied that it is accurate.

Terms of approval

It goes without saying that it is important to be clear and accurate when recording existing terms of approval. These should be taken word for word from the previous decision sheet. Within the review process, the decision-maker is required to consider whether any terms of approval remain appropriate.

Ethnicity

In recording a foster carer's ethnicity, it is expected that the supervising social worker will use the same terms that were used at the time of assessment; if the assessment was completed using Form F, then this will use the Office for National Statistics framework (see box below).

The Office for National Statistics framework to standardise the identification of an individual's ethnic background

White
1. English/Welsh/Scottish/Northern Irish/British
2. Irish
3. Gypsy or Irish Traveller
4. Any other White background, please describe

Mixed/Multiple ethnic groups
5. White and Black Caribbean
6. White and Black African
7. White and Asian
8. Any other Mixed/Multiple ethnic background, please describe

Asian/Asian British
9. Indian
10. Pakistani
11. Bangladeshi
12. Chinese
13. Any other Asian background, please describe

Black/African/Caribbean/Black British
14. African
15. Caribbean
16. Any other Black/African/Caribbean background, please describe

Other ethnic group
17. Arab
18. Any other ethnic group, please describe

For further details, see: www.ons.gov.uk/ons/guide-method/ measuring-equality/equality/ethnic-nat-identity-religion/ethnic-group/index.html#8

Child-minding

Some fostering services will have a policy that means foster carers are expected not to also child-mind. Others will be more flexible. If the foster carer is child-minding, it is important to provide information about this: the number of children, frequency and duration, and any comments about the impact of this on fostering.

Fostering review history

In completing this section, it is important to understand what is being asked. The date of initial approval is the date of the decision by the decision-maker that a person was deemed suitable to foster. It is not the date of the panel meeting that considered the assessment.

The date of the last fostering panel is self-explanatory, and it is recommended that the minutes from that meeting are attached to the supervising social worker report for information. This is especially useful if the review is going to be considered by the fostering panel because it is the first review, or for any other reason.

The date on which the last review was completed is the date that it was signed off by the fostering manager (using Form FR-H). It is not the date of the last review meeting, or the date of the last fostering panel.

DBS checks

Although it is not a legal requirement, many fostering services periodically update DBS checks, often on a three-yearly basis. However, changes to allow for online updates have made the process less costly and time-consuming, and there are now strong arguments to suggest that a DBS check should be updated as part of every foster carer review. This process might, for example, provide information about alcohol-related offences, or other information that would otherwise not have been reported to the fostering service.

Medical checks

This section provides an opportunity for very brief factual information only. Where more detailed information is needed about changes in carers' health, this can be included in the 'changes since last foster home review' section. Guidance about reviewing the health of foster carers is set out in Chapter 6.

Other checks

Although there is no requirement to undertake any other checks as part of the review process, some fostering services do update a number of the checks that were undertaken as part of the assessment, such as checks with health visitors and schools of birth children. If such checks are being routinely undertaken as part of the review process, it is important to be confident that these are useful and proportionate, bearing in mind that a lot of information about how foster carers are functioning can be ascertained from their day-to-day practice with fostered children.

Accommodation

This section requires some brief information about the foster home, setting out the number of bedrooms and who sleeps in each. If there are any room-sharing arrangements for children then this may need discussion, and there should be a description of each foster child's or young person's room. National Minimum Standard 10.6 states:

In the foster home, each child over the age of three should have their own bedroom. If this is not possible, the sharing of a bedroom is agreed by each child's responsible authority and each child has their own area within the bedroom. Before seeking agreement for the sharing of a bedroom, the fostering service provider takes into account any potential for bullying, any history of abuse or abusive behaviour, the wishes of the children concerned and all other pertinent facts.

The supervising social worker should always see a child's bedroom, and if this is in poor decorative state or not appropriately personalised, this may be an indication of how that child is perceived by the foster carer, and raises questions about whether the child's needs are being met.

Supervision arrangements

Foster care agreements are required to be put into place following approval and this constitutes a check that this has been done. Supervision agreements between supervising social workers and foster carers are recognised good practice and should cover the frequency of meetings and the practicalities about timings and who is expected to attend. The agreement should set out the purpose of supervision, the structure of the meeting (agenda), and arrangements for recording and agreeing conversations and actions. This section requires that dates of supervisory visits are recorded in relation to both foster carers (where relevant) to ensure that both foster carers are appropriately involved and supported.

Allegations and complaints

These sections ask for information about any allegations or complaints during the review period. There is space later in the form where the supervising social worker is expected to briefly summarise the fostering history, and within that is specifically asked to identify any themes or patterns that have emerged over time, including allegations, concerns and complaints (even where the veracity may be in doubt). Supervising social workers should use their judgement, and attach a chronology or placement record since approval, where appropriate.

Biehal *et al* (2014), looking at abuse and neglect in foster care, highlighted the importance of taking seriously the issue of allegations and complaints, making the point that warning signs were often missed. In 43 per cent of cases where allegations were substantiated, this followed previous unsubstantiated allegations, or a string of other low-level complaints, often by other children.

Past allegations and concerns about foster carers should be carefully recorded. Any new allegations that arise should be placed in historical context...A pattern of previous allegations, or simply concerns, about a foster carer should undoubtedly be viewed as a warning sign that should be taken seriously. In the 1990s, Utting's review of safeguarding for children living away from home noted that enquiries into abuse in foster care often uncover a background of previous allegations that had not been taken seriously. (Biehal *et al*, 2014, p 14; p 101)

Evidencing the Training, Support and Development Standards

Form FR is very deliberately structured to reflect the Training, Support and Development Standards (TSDS), and in most sections specifically asks the supervising social worker to 'describe and give examples'. This is crucial. The supervising social worker is not therefore expected to write that the foster carer meets all the child's health needs; but instead is expected to provide detailed information about *how* they do this.

For example, this might include descriptions of how the foster carer engaged with a particular child to talk about the importance of teeth brushing, demonstrated how to brush effectively, took them to the dentist, and subsequently set up a sticker chart to reward the child for good brushing. Or, in relation to working with professionals, specific information might relate to how a foster carer negotiated over potentially problematic contact plans, or how they prepared a particular child for a difficult review meeting.

Proposed change to approval terms

In considering this section, it is important that the supervising social worker does not simply assume that because things are going well, this means that existing approval terms are appropriate. It is important to achieve a good balance between having foster carers providing care for children whose needs they are best placed to meet, while at the same time not limiting placement opportunities by having too narrow terms of approval. As foster carers gain experience, and develop through training and supervision, it may be that whereas previously they felt unable to take more than one child, or children of a particular age, they increasingly feel that they could meet this challenge. In other cases, practical changes such as reduced working hours, or retirement, might mean that they have more time and so can take on more. Similarly, if health is deteriorating, or children of a particular age are proving too challenging, there is always scope to narrow approval terms. Supervising social workers need to be mindful of the links between inappropriate approval terms and subsequent fostering difficulties. Biehal *et al* note that in some cases of abuse and neglect, 'foster carers were evidently overstretched (taking on more children than they were approved to do or being required to mix very young children with older teenagers' (2014, p 130).

What is essential here is that any recommended change to terms of approval is accompanied by evidence to justify that change. If the type of fostering is to change from task-centred/short-term to permanent fostering, or to parent and child fostering, for example, it may be necessary to undertake further assessment of the foster carers, and the tools that are included with BAAF Prospective Foster Carer Report (Form F) (England) are very suitable for this purpose.

Similarly, if the foster carer wants to move to short break fostering for disabled children, for instance, then there might be benefits from providing additional assessment using the guidance notes that are included with Form F. Where foster carers want to move into other specialist fostering fields, this again may mean specific assessment to take account of the requirements of that role, and the fostering service will need to think about how best to present that information alongside the review.

Form FR-B: Foster carer report

In undertaking a foster carer review, Regulation 28(2) requires that the foster carer's views are sought and taken into account. Form FR-B is designed to meet that requirement, and consists of two parts.

- Part 1 is designed to be completed for all reviews and asks the carer to reflect on the period of fostering since the last review, and to think about what has changed during that period. It asks for information about working with others, and about training and development.

- Part 2 asks the foster carer to consider one or more of the children and young people they have fostered during the period and to think about how they have met their needs in line with some of the key aspects of the TSDS (see Chapter 5). While usually desirable, it is not essential that the foster carer completes Part 2, and local policy will need to set out whether this is required in all cases, in none, in some situations (for example, at the first review), or as a matter of judgement by the supervising social worker.

Where foster carers are fostering as a couple, it is expected that both carers should sign the report, although it is acceptable for one carer to complete it on behalf of them both, assuming that there is agreement about the content. These issues will need to be clearly set out in the letter that accompanies the form when it is sent out to the foster carer, and will need to reflect the specific requirements of the individual fostering service (see box overleaf). If the fostering service uses email or other electronic means to transfer information, then confidentiality and data protection issues must be carefully considered.

Example letter to foster carers

Dear [foster carer],

Please find attached Form FR-B that you are required to complete as part of your forthcoming foster carer review. Please can you complete Parts 1 and 2, and when referring to children and young people please use their initials and not full names.

If you are fostering as a couple, you are both required to sign the completed form, but if you agree on the content, then one of you can complete the form on behalf of you both. Please make sure that you complete all of the sections, even if at times this means writing 'not applicable'.

The completed form should be returned in the envelope provided to [address] no later than [date]. Please ensure that you adhere to this timescale so that the review process can run smoothly.

If you need any assistance in completing the form, or if you have any questions, please do not hesitate to contact your supervising social worker. Please do this at your earliest convenience so that the completion date is not missed.

Thank you in anticipation of your work in completing and returning this form.

Yours sincerely,

[Name and position]

[Name of fostering service]

Training and support

Because Form FR-B is based on the TSDS, the expectations of foster carers to complete these forms are very much in line with what is required in statutory guidance and in the National Minimum Standards. Nevertheless, some foster carers will need help and assistance, just as they do with completing the TSDS, and it is a matter for the fostering service to consider how best to provide this. It might be that where workshops are provided to assist with completing a TSDS workbook, then this will already cover the issues needed in completing this form, but fostering services may wish to consider providing something in the context of induction training or as a mandatory training session for foster carers within their first year of fostering. For some foster carers it will be necessary to supplement any formal training with one-to-one support, and this is most likely where carers lack confidence with written work, or where English is not their first language.

Form FR-B: Part 1

Health

In relation to the health update, it is important that the fostering service is aware of any changes or developments (see Chapter 6) and that information is conveyed fully and truthfully. At the same time, some medical information can be very personal, and in such circumstances it may be that the foster carer and supervising social worker need to agree how this can be worded in a way that maximises privacy and minimises embarrassment, but at the same time provides the recipient of the report with all the information that they need in considering the implications for fostering. In no circumstances should information be withheld or understated where this might conceivably be relevant in considerations about continued suitability to foster.

Working with others

Some sections in the form ask about working with other professionals: the supervising social worker, child's social worker, and others. This is an opportunity to consider whether the team around the child is working effectively, and for the foster carer to reflect on whether they are playing their part in this. It should be noted that foster carers are specifically asked about delegated authority and whether that has been used appropriately.

Develop yourself

In this part of the report there are separate sections pertaining to each foster carer (if they are fostering as a couple). It is important to recognise the requirement for all foster carers to participate in appropriate training and development and the fostering service will normally have a policy that sets out the specific local requirements in this regard. Where foster carers have done little to develop their knowledge, skills and understanding, or have not met the fostering service training requirement, then this will need further discussion within the review meeting.

Terms of approval

It is important that foster carers understand their terms of approval, and realise that they cannot lawfully take children outside of those terms for periods exceeding six working days. Good practice demands that fostering services comply with the law in this respect, but also that foster carers understand their responsibilities.

Form FR-B: Part 2

Where a fostering service requires Part 2 to be completed, this relates to children and young people, and asks foster carers to provide evidence in the form of a few examples. It is important that the foster carer understands that he or she is not required to simply state that they do certain things, or to provide vague generalisations about what they do, but instead are expected to give detailed and specific examples of work with the children they have cared for. This reflects exactly what is required of them in relation to achieving the TSDS, and some foster carers may need to be supported with this.

In other words, it is not enough for the foster carer to state: 'We provide leisure opportunities for Jay' or 'We always talk to Jay about getting involved in activities'. Instead, the foster carer might write:

> Jay was initially reluctant to get involved in any outside leisure activities and preferred to stay around at home. He did like helping with the gardening though, and we bought some children's gardening books and then located a local gardening club for children. He agreed to go with one of us for the first few sessions, but soon made a friend, and after that was happy to attend on his own each week.

Form FR-C: Sons and daughters comments

It is generally accepted (Hojer *et al*, 2013) that sons and daughters of foster carers play an important role in fostering. For some of them, living with foster children is a wholly or largely positive experience, but for others it is more challenging. Negative aspects can include having to share parental time and affection with other children, having to share toys and property, and at times having to witness or experience difficult behaviour. For Hojer *et al* (2013, p 5):

> The children and young people in carers' families need to be involved in family discussions concerning the decision to foster and should not be seen as less significant, passive members of the family.

They also need to be included in considerations about whether to continue fostering, and so it is important that their voices are clearly heard within the review process. At times it might seem to sons and daughters of foster carers that it is fostered children whose needs are dominant, and it is not by coincidence that Form FR is structured so that the views of sons and daughters follow immediately after their parents, reflecting their importance as part of the fostering family.

In identifying the potential challenges for children of foster carers, Hojer *et al* (2013, p 5) suggest that:

> One factor improving the capacity to cope was the opportunity to have open discussions about perceived difficulties, primarily with their parents, but also with social workers. If children and young people were allowed to complain about the things that they found problematic with fostering and were enabled to display negative feelings, they were better equipped to cope with problems.

This serves to emphasise the importance of meaningfully involving sons and daughters in the foster carer review process.

Using Form FR-C

In developing and piloting Form FR, it was impossible to achieve a consensus about what the forms for children should look like. While for some there was much to be said for simplicity and straightforward presentation, for others a more sophisticated approach was necessary to allow engagement with children and young people. It was ultimately decided that Form FR-C would emphasise the former, but it is important for fostering services to be aware that if they are unhappy with these forms, or have developed forms that they consider superior, then there is nothing to prevent them using those alternative forms instead (these should be reproduced on the fostering service's own headed paper).

Form FR-C consists of forms for the younger sons and daughters (C1: child), and for the older sons and daughters (C2: young person). They are broadly similar in that both ask sons and daughters what they like about fostering; what, if anything, they would like to change; and to whom they would talk if they were worried. The difference is that for the children (C1), there is an opportunity to draw a picture, and there is space for comments from an adult where the child needed to be assisted to complete the form. For the young people (C2), consent is sought to share the completed form with their parents. The supervising social worker can use their judgement in deciding which form is best suited to each child, and this will depend more on the development stage than the chronological age of the child or young person.

If there are other non-fostered children or young people living in the household, such as grandchildren or children subject to orders such as special guardianship, then it may be entirely appropriate for them to use Form FR-C. This will be a matter of judgement for the supervising social worker. It should be noted that neither of these forms is designed to be completed by adult children in the foster home; Form FR-F2 is more suitable for this purpose.

A note on formats

The FR-C forms are supplied as both PDF files and Word documents. The PDFs reflect an effort to improve the presentation of children's forms, but to save a completed form in PDF requires that it is filled in using a computer that has full Adobe Acrobat software. If a computer has only Adobe Reader, the forms can be completed and printed out, but they cannot be saved. For this reason, the two forms are supplied in Word as well as PDF formats. The Word versions should not have any compatibility issues, but are less visually appealing. Each fostering service will need to decide how best to manage this issue, depending on their own IT capacity.

Direct work with children

Wherever possible, both forms are designed to be completed by sons and daughters of foster carers in their own words and with the minimum of adult involvement. For many children, and for most young people, this will be relatively straightforward, but for others they may benefit from support, and this should always be offered. Where a fostering service operates support groups for sons and daughters of foster carers, it can be helpful to discuss this issue there, and to consider local practice in the light of any feedback provided.

More often, however, support will need to be provided on an individual basis, and this should be the responsibility of the supervising social worker to either offer directly, or to provide an appropriate adult to undertake this. Ideally, this person should be someone known to the child, and who they feel comfortable with. It is not appropriate for the foster carer to undertake this role, as children and young people need to feel able to share their views without worrying about the impact on their parents. There are a number of helpful publications that might assist supervising social workers and others in communicating effectively with children, including sons and daughters of foster carers, such as Lefevre (2010), Thomas (2009), and Luckock and Lefevre (2008).

With young children or children with additional needs, it may be that what they are able to write or draw does not fully reflect the content or feelings of what they conveyed in the session where they were supported by the supervising social worker, or other adult. For these situations, there is a section on the form where the supervising social worker or other adult can provide additional comments to give the recipient of the report a better sense of what the child or young person conveyed verbally, or non-verbally, or was trying to convey. This might involve some interpretation or speculation, but it is important to focus on trying to provide the child's own views and not those of the supervising social worker; these should already be fully contained in Form FR-A.

Form FR-D: Fostered child's and young person's comments

In undertaking a foster carer review, Regulation 28(3)(b) requires the fostering service to seek and take into account the views of any child or young person who is placed with the foster carer, subject to that child's age and understanding. Good practice suggests that the same goes for any child or young person who has been placed with the foster carer during the review period, but is no longer placed with them.

The general requirement to listen to children is further emphasised in the Fostering Services National Minimum Standards, and it is specifically required that 'the wishes, feelings and views of children are taken into account in monitoring foster carers' (NMS 1.7). Children should be encouraged to 'communicate their views on all aspects of their care' (NMS 1.3) and these views should be sought regularly (NMS 1.4). Without being able to understand how the foster home is experienced by children and young people living there, it is impossible to undertake a meaningful review:

> A foster child's contribution to a foster carer's review is key to the overall evaluation of the quality of foster care being provided. The foster child's experience of being cared for by the foster carer is fundamentally important. Without their contribution the review will only ever be partial. (Cosis Brown, 2011, p 64)

It is of concern that Biehal et al (2014) reveal that abuse in foster care often took place over many years, and often only came to light after the placement ended, because the children being subjected to that abuse felt unable to share their concerns. They point out that 'Risks of nondisclosure can be heightened when children lack opportunities to confide in social workers and the monitoring and review of placements, even apparently settled placements, are insufficient' (2014, p 13).

Using Form FR-D

Cosis Brown (2011, p 63) uses the term "contribution" rather than "report" to describe the input of the child or young person, emphasising that it is the content of what they want to convey that matters, not the format in which that information is provided. Although the FR-D forms are designed specifically to help children convey their views, the same goal can be achieved by using other approaches. It is important for fostering services to be aware that there is nothing to prevent them from using alternative forms if they prefer, or to provide the child's views using another format entirely. In deciding what is most appropriate, the supervising social worker and child's social worker should consider the needs of the individual child and, where appropriate, seek their views on this.

Form FR-D consists of forms for the younger age range (D1: fostered child's comments), and for the older age range (D2: fostered young person's comments). They are broadly similar in that both ask very general and open-ended questions about what the child or young person likes about living with their foster carers, how the foster carers have helped them, what they would like foster carers and social workers to do differently, and to whom they would talk if they were unhappy.

The main difference is that for the children (D1), there is an opportunity to draw a picture, and there is space for comments from an adult where the child needed to be assisted to complete the form. For the young people (D2), there are 12 specific statements that they are asked to agree or disagree with, and consent is sought to share the completed form with the foster carers. The supervising social worker can use their judgement in deciding which form is best suited to which child or young person; this will depend more on their developmental stage than their chronological age.

A note on formats

The FR-D forms are supplied as both PDF files and Word documents. The PDFs reflect an effort to improve the presentation of children's forms, but to save a completed form in PDF requires that it is filled in using a computer that has full Adobe Acrobat software. If a computer has only Adobe Reader, the forms can be completed and printed out, but they cannot be saved. For this reason, the two forms are supplied in Word as well as PDF formats. The Word versions should not have any compatibility issues, but are less visually appealing. Each fostering service will need to decide how best to manage this issue, depending on their own IT capacity.

Practice issues

In planning the review, the supervising social worker will need to consider the most appropriate method for ascertaining the views and wishes of the child or young person. Wherever possible, it is desirable for the child or young person to complete the form in his or her own words; this will convey the genuine feeling in a way that is likely to be lost if the sentiment is summarised by another person. Sometimes a child or young person will prefer to complete the form with minimal adult involvement; others will need considerable support in order to be able to make a meaningful contribution.

If support is required, then consideration will need to be given as to who is best placed to provide this. This should never be the foster carer, as the child is being expected to comment on him or her, and the care that is provided in the foster home. Usually the most suitable person will be either the child's social worker or the supervising social worker; however, there may be others who are well placed to facilitate this, such as a support worker from the fostering service. Whoever undertakes this role should be familiar to the child or young person, and also someone whom they can trust. There are a number of helpful texts that might assist supervising social workers and others in communicating effectively with children, such as Lefevre (2010), Thomas (2009), and Luckock and Lefevre (2008).

If the child or young person is being supported to make a contribution, then the forms should be used as a tool for conversation and recording, and be utilised flexibly in line with whatever the child wishes to convey. The questions are deliberately general and open-ended for the most part, and while some children will be able to write in answers, others will be happier providing verbal responses. For some children, it may be that drawing a picture is enough, but every effort should be made to seek some sort of contribution wherever that is possible. It is important that supervising social workers and others do not assume that, just because a child is young or has additional needs, they are incapable of expressing a view about how they experience fostering. Some fostering services have demonstrated an ability to seek such views in a meaningful way, but this will depend on a commitment to do this, and an organisational culture that expects it.

There is space on the child's form for comments from the person assisting the child, and this should be used to help the reader make sense of whatever information the child has provided. The adult may wish to use this space to provide basic information about how the session was conducted, and if verbal comments from a child were entered by the adult, to be clear about this. It may be appropriate to comment on the child's non-verbal communication during the session, and to offer any observations about this. However, it is important that this section remains focused on conveying the child's views; there are other forms designed to elicit the views of the various adults.

In seeking information in the review from children and young people no longer living in the foster home, it may be best to have processes that routinely collect their views around the time the placement is ending, when the issues feel relevant and current. However, that may not always be appropriate or possible, and sometimes having time for reflection allows for a fairer and more considered assessment. If the child or young person has since moved to another placement, it will usually be necessary to ask their social worker to seek their views. This will be particularly important where the placement ended in an unplanned way or where there were particular difficulties during the time the child or young person was living with the foster carer.

Form FR-E: Child's social worker report

In undertaking a foster carer review, Regulation 28(3)(b) requires the fostering service to seek and take into account the views of the placing authority for any child placed with the foster carer in the preceding year, and statutory guidance has clarified that in practice this means seeking the views of the social worker for that child. This legal position is stated as a note at the start of Form FR-E so that this is clear to the child's social worker, who may be less familiar with fostering legislation than the supervising social worker.

In addition to being a legal requirement, the child's social worker views are essential in ensuring that the review is thorough and complete. Hearing from the person who effectively commissions the foster carer on behalf of the child means that any collusion (deliberate or unintended) between the supervising social worker and the foster carer to present things as better than they are is not possible, and that if the child feels unable to fully set out their concerns (as they are living in that home), then their social worker can do it for them. In this respect, the child's social worker has a crucial safeguarding responsibility.

More than this, however, the child's social worker is also uniquely placed to comment on how well the foster carer is able to work with professional colleagues, to work with the foster child's birth family, and to participate effectively in meetings such as child care reviews. Where the child's social worker has a different perspective to the supervising social worker – for better or worse – this is important and needs to be taken seriously.

Using Form FR-E

It is recognised that children's social workers are under considerable stress, often with large caseloads and competing priorities. Both local authority and independent fostering services often report struggling to get child's social work reports completed. Form FR-E was devised with this very much in mind, consisting primarily of a "yes/no" set of nine questions with additional comments being optional. The guidance notes at the top of the form recognise the need to have realistic expectations:

Children's social workers are expected to complete these reports, but the time that goes into this needs to be proportionate. Supervising social workers will be writing the main in-depth reports that provide evidence about the foster carer's practice, and these will be supplemented by a combination of "yes/no" answers and/or any additional brief comments from the child's social worker.

If the foster carer has performed well then a fairly brief report is acceptable. If the child's social worker has answered "no" to any of the questions, and is concerned about the foster carer's practice, then they will need to write more in order to convey these concerns clearly. It is not acceptable for the child's social worker to not complete the form at all.

The key point here is that supervising social workers must be responsible for the vast bulk of information that is provided as part of the review process; the child's social work report is designed to supplement that.

Practice issues

Sometimes children's social workers do not complete reports as requested because they are satisfied that all is going well, and they consider that writing a report to this effect is not an effective use of their time. That position is understandable, except for the fact that it is perfectly possible to complete the form in less than five minutes by simply confirming that the foster carer meets the standards set out in Form FR-E (by circling "yes" for each of the nine items) and providing a sentence to acknowledge the foster carer's good work over the year. At times the child's social worker may not realise that they can comply with the request that easily, and so the supervising social worker may need to point this out.

Some fostering services find that the most effective way to obtain the information they require is for supervising social workers or administrators to telephone the child's social worker and seek the information verbally over the telephone. This is an entirely appropriate approach when things are straightforward and positive, and where this has been the technique used, a completed version of the form should be emailed back to the social worker to confirm their view. It must also be made clear on the form that the information has been provided verbally, and it may be that the supervising social worker or administrator makes a note to this effect in the signature box.

In other circumstances, it may be that the child's social worker does not complete the form as requested because they are dissatisfied with the foster carer's performance and do not wish to get involved in lengthy arguments about the merit of their views. This is more difficult to resolve, but social workers do need to understand that any identified poor practice can only be addressed if concerns are fully shared, and at times they cannot avoid becoming embroiled in these discussions. In this context, it is not appropriate for administrators to try to obtain verbal feedback, and where children's social workers have concerns they must be encouraged to take responsibility for putting these in writing.

Children's social workers will be most likely to engage with the process if they feel that the fostering service is competent and committed to addressing identified shortcomings in the foster carer's practice. The supervising social worker may need to offer explanations to this effect, and to provide assurances regarding the independent nature of the review meeting and panel process.

Matters can become particularly problematic if the supervising social worker does not accept concerns put forward by the child's social worker, but that does not make those concerns any less important. Instead, it requires careful consideration of the different perspectives through the review process, and may indicate the benefit of fostering panel scrutiny.

In situations where a child's social worker is not responding to repeated requests for an appropriate contribution, the onus must be on the fostering service to be proactive in following this up. In the first instance, that might be through an administrator or supervising social worker, but if those efforts fail, then a senior manager will need to become involved to ensure that statutory requirements are met, and that any potential safeguarding concerns are fully addressed.

Sometimes the difficulty relates to the fact that there is a relatively new social worker who has only recently met the foster carer, or the case may be allocated to a manager who has limited involvement. In these situations, it is important that reference is made to the case records that the social worker will have maintained, and that a form is completed accordingly. Such issues also highlight the benefits of completing the forms at the point at which any placement ends, as this reduces the risk of the social worker having moved on by the time of the foster carer review.

Form FR-F: Additional reports

When undertaking a foster carer review, Regulation 28(1)(a) requires the fostering service to 'make such enquiries and obtain such information as they consider necessary' in order to reach a view about the continued suitability of the foster carer and their household. Practice is varied in this regard, with some fostering services seeking a range of information from third parties, and others seeking very little or none. Clearly, where more information is available, and from a wide range of sources, this will mean that the review is more detailed, and the risk of omissions or professional collusion will be reduced.

Form FR-F consists of four forms, as follows:

- FR-F1: other professionals

- FR-F2: adult household member/support to foster carer

- FR-F3: birth parent/birth family member

- FR-F4: parent in parent and child arrangement

Which of these forms are used will depend on the individual circumstances of each fostering household, the type of fostering they are engaged in, and the policy of that fostering service.

Form FR-F1: Other professionals

This form, as the title suggests, is for feedback from professionals other than the supervising social worker or child's social worker. It might be that reports are sought from the foster child's school, nursery or health visitor, youth offending worker, mentor, or CAMHS worker. In some circumstances, it may also be appropriate to seek a report from a Children's Guardian, and where the foster carer has been involved in moving a child to adoption, the prospective adopters may be well placed to provide useful information. It may also be appropriate to ask the Independent Reviewing Officer for their views, and this can be particularly useful if the social worker's views are limited or unavailable.

Different fostering services will have different expectations in this regard, and this should be set out in their policy about the conduct of reviews. However, where other professionals have raised concerns about the foster carer's practice, then they should always be asked to provide written information for the review.

Where issues relating to birth children have caused difficulties, concerns or challenges during the review period, consideration should also be given to contacting professionals involved with that child, and asking them to provide written information. Depending on the particular issues, it might be appropriate to use Form FR-F1 for this purpose, or it might be necessary to ask specific questions of that professional. Some fostering services routinely contact agencies such as the schools of birth children. Where this is the case, that fostering service should have reached a view that this is useful and proportionate, and will have developed a specific form for that purpose.

It goes without saying that whatever reports are being sought for the review, this should be clear to the foster carer in terms of being the routine expectation of the fostering service (and set out in policy that has been provided to the foster carer) or should be specific to their situation and agreed with him or her individually. It would not be appropriate for the fostering service to seek reports when or if the foster carer was unaware that this was happening.

In seeking information from other professionals, Form FR-F1 very clearly focuses on the foster carer, and not the child who is the service user. In other words, what is important is not, for example, whether the child is making good progress at school, but how the foster carer is supporting that progress. Or, if the child has particular problems, it is important that the foster carer is not judged on this, but rather on how he or she is working with others to try and address these problems.

Form FR-F1 specifically seeks permission from the person providing the report to share that information with the foster carer, and this is also addressed in the example letter to professionals (see text box overleaf).

Example letter to other professional

Dear [name of other professional],

Re: [name of subject child]

You may be aware that the parent/carer of this child is a foster carer for [name of fostering service]. We are required to review the suitability of every foster home on an annual basis, and as part of that process we contact people who may have relevant information to share.

We would be very grateful if you would be willing to complete the enclosed Form FR-F1. If this form is not helpful in allowing you to provide the information that you want to give, then please feel free to attach additional pages or to provide information in another way.

The completed form or other comments should be returned in the envelope provided to [address] no later than [date]. Please could you adhere to this timescale as the various review papers are collated in advance of a review meeting that is held shortly after this date.

Form FR-F1 asks for you to consent to the report being shared with the foster carer, and in order that we can fully discuss matters with foster carers in an open and transparent way, we expect that professionals will routinely give this consent. Without a willingness to share information, it is very difficult to address any concerns that you might have.

Please be aware that if you raise matters of a child protection nature it may be necessary to share these concerns with foster carers even if you do not want this; and depending on the nature of the concerns, the foster carers may be able to ascertain where the information has come from. When referring to children and young people in your response please use their initials and not their full names.

If you need any assistance in completing the form, or if you have any questions, including questions about the sharing of information with the foster carer(s), please do not hesitate to contact me (at your earliest convenience to allow us time to address any matters you may have).

Thank you in anticipation of your assistance. The foster carer review process is an important way in which we ensure that our foster carers are effective in meeting the needs of children in care.

Yours sincerely,

[Name and position]

[Name of fostering service]

Form FR-F2: Adult household member/support to foster carer

Adult household members, who are often but not always the foster carer's birth children, can play a very important role in the success or otherwise of a foster placement (Sinclair, 2005, p 84). However, while some adult household members will be active in fostering, others will be living very independent lives and will be little impacted. It may be that the foster carer's parent or parents are sharing their home, and they may be a significant help in fostering, or may require care themselves. It is important that the fostering service has a good understanding of the role these individuals play, and that they are invited to share their perspective on living in a fostering household.

Some fostering services ask foster carers to nominate people to support them in their fostering task, and it may be that these people are included in the initial assessment of the foster carer's suitability, or may even be assessed in their own right regarding their suitability to support the foster carers. Where foster carers do have a "nominated supporter" or some equivalent, then this individual or couple should be asked to complete Form FR-F2 as part of the fostering review process for the foster carer whom they are linked to. The only exception to this might be where they have a dedicated review process of their own. It is not anticipated that people in the foster carer's general support network should be routinely contacted, only those who have some formalised role in supporting foster carers.

Form FR-F2 provides a simple structure for all adult household members (including unrelated members like lodgers) and for formal supporters to identify the positive and negative aspects of fostering, and to highlight any issues for the fostering service to consider.

Consideration will need to be given to the practicalities of distributing these forms according to the specific circumstances of each case. In some cases, it will be best to do this in person; in others, by email or letter. Whatever method is used, it will be necessary to offer the opportunity for a conversation with the supervising social worker if required, and the recipient will need to be aware of the date by which the completed response is required.

One group that is worth considering are young people, usually birth children, who may be away at college or university but are also living in the foster home and returning for holiday periods. If they are not at home at the time of the review, it may be tempting to omit them from the process, but best practice is to seek their views by emailing the form or seeking their views in another way.

Form FR-F3: Birth parent/birth family member

Although there is no legal requirement to seek the views of the foster child's parents as part of the foster carer review process, this is recommended by the UK National Standards (UK Joint Working Party on Foster Care, 1999) and constitutes good practice. This is routine in some fostering services, and clearly demonstrates a commitment to working in partnership with the birth family, and seeking user feedback. Seeking views from a wide range of perspectives increases the information available about the foster carer's practice and allows the reader of the report to compare the perspective of different parties.

Birth parents will often be particularly well placed to comment on whether the foster carer is promoting contact with them, and their views should be considered alongside the views offered by the supervising social worker and child's social worker, as well as from the child themselves. There may also be circumstances when it is appropriate to seek information from other family members such as grandparents, adult siblings, or aunts and uncles. The supervising social worker will need to make a judgement about this according to the specifics of the case.

There will clearly be some circumstances where it is not appropriate to seek the views of birth parents, such as where the child has effectively been abandoned and there is no contact, since in this scenario the birth parents will not be in a position to offer informed comments. However, in the majority of cases, the birth parent will have something to say. Just because they may be antagonistic, or looking to criticise, this is not good reason for excluding them from the process. If criticism is unfair, then this should be evident from the other reports and information that are available as part of the foster carer review.

The supervising social worker will need to think carefully about how best to contact birth parents, and should consult with the child's social worker about this. In some cases, it will be appropriate to post Form FR-F3 with a covering letter; in other cases, contact via email might be best; and in yet other cases, the social worker might pass on the form in person. Whatever method is used, the birth parent should also be offered the alternative of talking with a social worker in person or by telephone; this might be particularly important where the parent has limited literacy skills, or where English is not their first language. In those situations, the social worker may still wish to use Form FR-F3 to structure and record the discussion, but should clearly note on the form the extent of their involvement.

Example letter to birth parent

Dear [birth parent],

You will be aware that your child [or children] are being [or have been] looked after by [name of foster carer] who is a foster carer for [name of fostering service]. I am the social worker for that foster carer.

We are required to review the suitability of every foster home on an annual basis, and as part of that process we contact parents of fostered children to get their views.

We would therefore be very grateful if you would be willing to complete the enclosed Form FR-F3. The completed form should be returned in the envelope provided to [address] no later than [date]. If you do not reply by this date, then your views cannot be considered as part of this review.

The form asks you to allow us to share your comments with the foster carer, as without this it is very difficult to address any concerns that you might have. Please be aware that if you raise matters of a child protection nature, it may be necessary to share these concerns with foster carers even if you do not want this.

If you need any help in completing the form, or would prefer to meet with someone or speak on the telephone, please contact me [or name of social worker] at your earliest convenience to allow us time to arrange this before the foster carer review meeting.

Thank you for your help. The foster carer review process is an important way in which we ensure that our foster carers are doing a good job in meeting the needs of children in foster care.

Yours sincerely,

[Name and position]

[Name of fostering service]

Form FR-F4: Parent in parent and child arrangement

Parent and child fostering is a very specific type of fostering (see Adams and Dibben, 2011) and Form FR-F4 has been designed specifically for use with parents in this situation. It asks the parent to identify the positive aspects of the placement and to identify anything they would like the foster carer to do differently. It also checks that information has been provided about how to make a complaint. Consent is sought for sharing the information with the foster carer.

Providing the form to the parent should be relatively straightforward as they will be living in the foster home. However, it is important that the supervising social worker and the child's social worker agree about who will talk to the parent about completing the form, and who will offer support if this is required. As with a birth parent who is living away from their child, it is important to recognise that issues of literacy or language may impact on their ability to complete the form unassisted.

Form FR-G: Reviewing officer report

Although there is no legal requirement to involve a reviewing officer or to hold a review meeting, any process that does not have this in place will be unable to achieve the full benefits of a comprehensive foster carer review. Standard 16.6 of the UK National Standards (UK Joint Working Party on Foster Care, 1999) suggests that:

> A review meeting is held that includes the carer and the supervising social worker, and is chaired by an appropriate third party, who can form an independent judgement and is knowledgeable about foster care.

Cosis Brown (2011, p 78) explains why this part of the review process is so important:

> The foster carer review meeting offers the opportunity for the foster carer, social worker and reviewing officer to consider in detail and depth the quality of the fostering that has been undertaken during a review period thus enabling an evaluation to be made of the quality of that foster care. The review meeting is where differences of view, concerns and areas for further development can be explicitly discussed and plans made about how they will be addressed. The review meeting is a forum in which a foster carer's work can be appraised and where examples of good and excellent work can be identified.

It is difficult to overstate the importance of this meeting; it is where the various reports and comments are brought together in one place and evaluated, allowing for reflection and development. It is also an opportunity for foster carers to share their experiences of the fostering service, to provide feedback, and to address any particular issues that are frustrating them. A robust and comprehensive review process that includes an independently chaired meeting is likely to correlate with a low level of complaints and allegations, as potential difficulties can be identified and addressed at an early stage.

Some fostering services will employ dedicated reviewing officers, and others will use Independent Reviewing Officers for this role. Sometimes a fostering service will contract with individual self-employed practitioners, and some will use managers within their own fostering services. Whatever the local arrangements are, it is important that anyone undertaking this role is genuinely independent, which means that they are not line managers of the supervising social workers, or members of their team; nor should they be involved in reviewing the cases of the particular children who are placed with those foster carers.

While fostering panel involvement can bring considerable benefits in terms of the scrutiny and independent monitoring of reviews, it is important to recognise that this process is something separate and different to the review meeting. The panel meeting cannot reasonably be used as an alternative to a review meeting, and as Cosis Brown points out, 'a proper in-depth exploration about the quality of a foster carer's practice cannot be conducted in a fostering panel forum' (2011, p 53). However effective a fostering panel might be, it cannot compensate for an inadequate review process. The review and the panel are very different, with structures and processes that serve very different purposes.

The review meeting

In preparing for the review meeting, it is recommended that the completed reports (Form FR-A to FR-F) are available to the reviewing officer at least two weeks before the review meeting. This will allow the reviewing officer time to seek any clarifications or request further information where there are obvious gaps in the paperwork. The reviewing officer should also have access to the previous review meeting record and the last set of minutes from the fostering panel and, depending on the issues raised in the paperwork, may wish to look at the foster carer's assessment report. Having read the papers, the reviewing officer should be in a position to set an individualised agenda for the meeting that addresses issues that have been raised by both the foster carer and the supervising social worker.

It will be a matter for individual reviewing officers as to exactly how they conduct the review meeting, but it will need to consider:

- whether recommendations made at the previous review have been acted upon;

- any significant changes for the foster carers and their family since the last review;

- whether checks and other requirements are up to date and completed in line with the policy of the fostering service;

- the impact of fostering on any birth children in the family;

- the quality of the care provided to fostered children and young people and the extent to which their needs have been met;

- working relationships with the fostering service and others, including other professionals and birth families;

- the foster carer's training and development over the review period and for the future;

- the support that is available to the foster carer and any feedback that they may have for the fostering service;

- whether the foster carer's terms of approval are appropriate or whether they need to be changed.

The review must be a robust meeting that serves as an important quality assurance mechanism for the fostering service, but it needs to be much more than a series of checklists, and to be useful needs to allow for in-depth discussion and reflection. Where the paperwork is of a high quality, it will be relatively easy for the reviewing officer to refer to particular areas for further discussion and reflection, but where it is less comprehensive, the reviewing officer may need to be more proactive in drawing out information. It is essential that any issues of identified poor practice are carefully considered, and any apparent inconsistencies explored. Cosis Brown (2011) provides more detailed consideration of how reviewing officers might manage these meetings.

Using Form FR-G

Form FR-G is designed so that parts can be completed in advance of the review meeting, and these are primarily the checklist-type elements. Where reports are not available that should be, the reviewing officer is expected to take action to acquire these, wherever possible, in advance of the review meeting. If problems are persistent in this regard, it may be that the reviewing officer will need to take this up with the fostering service. With regards to checks, medicals and other documents, each fostering service will have their own policies, and it is necessary for the reviewing officer to be familiar with these. It is anticipated that these parts of the form can also be completed in advance of the review, using material primarily in the supervising social worker report with any additional activity as might be required by local policies.

One specific section in the form asks the reviewing officer to check whether there were any exemptions granted or placements made outside of approval terms for longer than six days (unlawful placements). The law requires that this should never be the case, and where it emerges that approval terms could properly be widened to allow the placement of particular children, this can be lawfully achieved through holding a review within the first six days of the emergency placement. However, in practice some fostering services do not routinely achieve this, and make unlawful placements at times. It is well recognised that in these circumstances there is a heightened risk of placement breakdowns or other difficulties (see Biehal *et al*, 2014, p 130), and reviewing officers are well placed to help fostering services and foster carers understand their responsibilities in this regard.

The discussion section of the form is deliberately largely unstructured, to allow reviewing officers considerable flexibility in how they present information from the review. Reviewing officers are asked to report under the broad headings of:

● Impact of fostering

● Needs of children

● Working as part of a team

● Carer's own development

It should be specifically noted that, within the brief guidance notes contained in the form, reviewing officers are asked to consider how delegated authority is working, as this is recognised to be an area of particular challenge. In relation to the carer's own development, this is purposely separated so that if there is more than one foster carer, they are considered as individuals in this respect.

The final section of the form asks the reviewing officer to summarise strengths, concerns and areas for development, bringing together all the information and highlighting any differences of opinion or perspective. It is then necessary to consider terms of approval (see discussion in Chapter 2) and to proactively consider whether widening or narrowing the approval terms might be desirable. This involves considerations that take into account the need for foster carers to be available for the widest range of children and young people, but only if they have the skills and circumstances that will allow them to meet their needs effectively, and where they have the appropriate level of support.

Form FR-H: Fostering service manager report

Regulation 28(4) states that, 'At the conclusion of the review, the fostering service must prepare a written report', and this can be done using Form FR-H. This is a crucial report in that it constitutes the end of the review process, and it is suggested that the date on which this is signed is recognised as the date that the review was completed. The term "fostering service manager" in this context should be interpreted as the line manager for the supervising social workers; it is not anticipated that a more senior (and remote) manager should be responsible for this, although that must ultimately be a decision for the individual fostering service.

Form FR-H is expected to be a short form that, in most circumstances, is simple to complete. It asks for the recommendation, reasons and any comments, and it is anticipated that in most cases this will involve cross-referencing to other parts of the report. Only if the manager has a different opinion to that of the supervising social worker or reviewing officer will they need to provide detailed written explanations, or if there are particular complexities that need explanation.

If the processes suggested in this guide have been followed, the fostering service manager will have seen and agreed the supervising social worker report, and potentially other reports, at an earlier stage, and should be aware of the issues under consideration in each particular case. They should also be familiar with the case from supervision meetings. It is therefore anticipated that in most cases they should be able to read the various reports and complete Form FR-H within about half an hour. This suggests that there is no excuse for delays at this stage in the process.

It is suggested that the fostering service manager complete Form FR-H within two weeks of receipt, although usually it should be unnecessary to utilise this full period. A prompt response in relation to finalising the review process will mean that when papers are passed to the decision-maker or fostering panel, the information will be current and up to date, and this will also maximise opportunity in meeting any deadlines for panel papers. If the fostering service manager fails to complete the form within the two-week period, there is the risk that the review will not be completed within the required timescale.

Form FR-I: Decision sheet

The decision sheet (Form FR-I) is designed for use by the fostering service decision-maker and, if used correctly, will meet all the requirements established in *Hofstetter v LB Barnet and IRM* [2009] EWCA 328 (Admin). It can be used for cases whether or not the fostering panel has been involved in making a recommendation.

Discussions about the role of the fostering panel in considering reviews are set out in detail elsewhere (Borthwick and Lord, 2011; Cosis Brown, 2011), including the legal requirement for the panel to be involved in considering first reviews. Wherever it is possible, panel involvement in considering reviews must be seen as a potentially beneficial arrangement, and where resources permit, the panel should consider all reviews. Where this is not achievable, it may be helpful for the panel to consider reviews on a three-yearly basis, and/or in relation to individual cases where changes of approval are being proposed, or where concerns have been raised.

In practice, it is anticipated that Form FR-I may be part-completed by the fostering service manager (or an administrator on their behalf) before it is passed to the decision-maker. This is simply recognition that these individuals may be better placed to complete factual information including names and dates, and to copy and paste recommendations and reasons from fostering panel minutes or from the fostering service manager report (FR-H), and in no way suggests that the decision-maker should delegate their responsibility for making the decision or qualifying determination, which is not permissible under the legislation.

The decision-maker should independently complete other parts of the report that involve them making a judgement or decision or qualifying determination, and while they may cross-reference to other recommendations and reasons where these are shared and accepted, this must not be a "rubber stamping" exercise. The decision-maker must be able to defend and explain any reasoning that they have adopted, and be ultimately responsible for the decision or qualifying determination that is made.

Achieving the Training, Support and Development Standards (TSDS)

5

Introduction

The Children Act 1989 Guidance and Regulations Volume 4: Fostering Services (2011, paragraph 5.70) sets out the expectation that:

> *Foster carers should be supported to maintain an ongoing training and development portfolio which demonstrates how they are meeting the skills required of them. The foster carer must be able to evidence the Children's Workforce Development Council's Training, Support and Development Standards for Foster Care, within the timescales specified in Standard 20.*

National Minimum Standard 20 clarifies that:

- Foster carers must be supported to achieve the Children's Workforce Development Council's Training, Support and Development Standards for Foster Care within 12 months of approval.

- Family and friends foster carers must be supported to achieve the Children's Workforce Development Council's Training, Support and Development Standards for Family and Friends Foster Carers within 18 months of approval.

- Short break foster carers must be supported to achieve the Children's Workforce Development Council's Training, Support and Development Standards for Short Break Carers within 18 months of approval.

It should be noted that the Department for Education assumed responsibility for the TSDS after the Children's Workforce Development Council ceased to exist, and so the term "CWDC standards" is no longer accurate, although the statutory guidance and NMS have yet to be amended accordingly.

The evidence

Guidance from the Department for Education makes clear that evidence of meeting the TSDS can come from a range of sources. Considerable evidence should be available from attendance at the pre-approval fostering preparation training, and Fostering Network suggests that the Skills to Foster course covers 60 per cent of what is required in the TSDS. Additionally, there will be relevant material contained within the foster carer's assessment report (using Form F or an equivalent format) and in activity that was undertaken during the assessment process.

Form FR has been designed to provide significant further evidence of how foster carers meet the TSDS based on their practice and learning during the period following approval. Where appropriate within the forms, the specifically relevant standards are noted, and this should assist the supervising social worker in being able to identify where issues have been covered and where they have not. This will be particularly important during the first year of fostering and the completed review can be used as a major source of evidence to show that the standards have been achieved as required.

While most fostering services use a workbook to compile evidence regarding the TSDS, this is not strictly necessary, and OFSTED guidance to their inspectors (2011) makes clear that they do not need to see foster carers' workbooks. Instead, fostering services might choose to provide their evidence in a different way, and it is envisaged that the vast majority of the evidence should be available from three broad sources:

● a comprehensive pre-approval training programme;

● a detailed and carefully constructed assessment report;

● a rigorous foster carer review using Form FR.

The extent to which Form FR provides satisfactory evidence will of course be dependent on how well each section is completed, but it may be that practitioners and foster carers make a particular effort to provide extensive information at year one, and reduce this slightly in subsequent years.

The process

If a fostering service were to use the materials identified as an alternative to individual workbooks, they would need to carefully map the evidence against a TSDS grid for each individual foster carer, to make sure that each and every standard was covered satisfactorily. Where gaps remain – the extent of these gaps will depend on the quality of the preparation training and the individual circumstances of the carer both pre- and post-approval – these will need to be filled. Potentially, this can be done by a combination of attendance at training and other learning, such as e-learning or completion of exercises and worksheets.

Since the first foster carer review must be completed within a year of approval, this coincides with the 12-month timescale for achieving the standards as noted above (although short break and family and friends carers have a longer period of 18 months). This provides the obvious opportunity to run the two processes alongside each other, but the detail of exactly how this will work will depend on the specific arrangements within each individual fostering service.

If a fostering service preferred to continue with a workbook approach, then the review using Form FR would still be a significant source of good quality information that could be utilised by the foster carer.

6

Reviewing the foster carer's health

Introduction

Although there is no statutory requirement to review the health of foster carers, fostering services are required to 'make such enquiries and obtain such information as they consider necessary'. The foster carer review process provides an important opportunity to consider the health of the foster carer and family members, and to look at promoting healthy lifestyles. It is well recognised that fostering is stressful and challenging, and it is considerably easier to meet this challenge if the foster carer is in good physical and mental health.

Historically, the BAAF Health Group Advisory Committee has recommended that foster carers should have routine health reviews at two-yearly intervals, alternating between a comprehensive health assessment necessitating a visit to their GP (using Form AH), and a request for information from the carers and their GP (using Form AH2). However, this approach overlooked the importance of ongoing monitoring and support regarding health concerns of carers, and tended to place the responsibility for health matters on health professionals rather than this being shared with social care professionals and foster carers themselves.

This has led to discussions involving three BAAF groups – the Health Group Advisory Committee, the UK Social Work Practice Advisory Committee and the Independent Fostering Providers Forum – that have considered more collaborative approaches to monitoring health which meet legal and good practice requirements. In considering the health of foster carers, it is widely accepted that there are a number of principles that should inform practice.

Good practice principles

- All prospective foster carers should be subject to the comprehensive health assessment process, including advice from a medical adviser during their original assessment.

- Foster carers should understand that it is their responsibility to inform their supervising social worker (or other members of the fostering service) about any changes to their health that might impact on their ability to foster, or might be perceived as likely to impact on their fostering.

- Similarly, supervising social workers should recognise that they have a responsibility to talk to foster carers about their health, and to raise any issues based on observations or other information provided to them. Best practice suggests that these discussions should take place in the context of a good professional relationship in which the foster carer feels valued and supported.

- The foster carer review should also consider the matter of the foster carer's health, and the foster carer and supervising social worker should be asked to comment on this. The fostering service might wish to consider the use of an annual health questionnaire.

- Where medical issues are identified at review, it is essential that non-medical professionals take advice from a medical adviser.

- When questions or concerns arise about health, there should always be an opportunity to seek further information from the foster carer's GP, relevant consultant or other qualified medical practitioner, to assess risks to health and parenting ability. Fostering services need to be reassured that foster carers are sufficiently healthy to undertake the fostering task, and to have information that allows them to effectively support the carer.

- At times, the medical adviser may recommend that a comprehensive health assessment be completed (using Form AH); this should not be perceived as criticism of the foster carer, and there should be an expectation that foster carers comply with this request where it is reasonably made.

- In cases where there is doubt or disagreement about the significance of health concerns, services should err on the side of caution and require that the assessment be undertaken, or a named consultant be contacted. A robust safeguarding approach should be taken, that recognises that fostering services need good information about the health of their foster carers.

- If at any point a condition is identified that could impair the carer's ability to care safely, then in addition to ongoing monitoring by the social worker, medical advice should be sought concerning how and when to conduct the next review of the carer's health.

- Fostering services should recognise that periods of ill health are the norm for many parents and carers, and wherever possible should be looking at how best to support foster carers in such circumstances. Any supportive arrangements will need to take account of the needs of any children placed, and will need to consider the likely prognosis and timescales in each individual set of circumstances.

- Fostering services should promote healthy lifestyles, ensuring that foster carers are provided with relevant information about smoking, alcohol use, diet, exercise, obesity and stress management.

Addressing health in Form FR

In line with these principles, Form FR-A asks the supervising social worker to provide information including the date of the last medical, the medical adviser's comments, and the date that any health questionnaire was completed. It also requires the supervising social worker to provide information about any changes in the carer's health in the section about 'changes since the last foster home review'. Form FR-B directly asks foster carers to answer the same question and asks them to identify how this has impacted on them and their family. Where appropriate, it would be expected that the reviewing officer will pick up on the issues and include a discussion about health within the review meeting.

Fostering service policy

Form FR-A notes that each fostering service will have their own written policy regarding the health of foster carers, and this should be developed in consultation with the medical adviser. The purpose of any such policy must be to ensure that foster carers are encouraged to live and promote a healthy lifestyle; to ensure that the fostering service is aware of any health concerns that may impact on the foster carer's ability to foster effectively; and to set out how the service might support foster carers who have short- or long-term ill-health.

The policy will also need to include whether there is a requirement for periodic health assessments or medicals, and whether or not foster carers are required to complete health questionnaires at set intervals. The BAAF Health Group Advisory Committee is working to develop a health questionnaire that might usefully be used as part of the foster carer review process, and it is hoped that this will become available before the end of 2014. In relation to the issue of periodic health assessments, discussions have not reached a consensus. For the BAAF Health Group Advisory Committee:

> A comprehensive health assessment with the carer's usual GP at regular intervals is a helpful part of a wider strategy, and these should occur at least every five years. This will act as a safeguard against health issues being under-reported or overlooked.

For other practitioners and members of other BAAF advisory groups, the routine nature of these assessments is undesirable, and, in line with the principles set out above, health assessments with the foster carer's GP should be arranged when circumstances suggest a need to do this. It will be a matter for individual fostering services to decide on what is right for their fostering service.

Fostering service policies

7

In order to run an effective system of foster carer reviews, each fostering service provider will need to have produced a series of policies and procedures to inform their practice. These will need to be drafted and agreed in accordance with local practice and it is inevitable that they will be determined by local managerial perspectives and preferences. It is not therefore appropriate for this guide to dictate what these policies should state, but this chapter highlights areas that need to be addressed, and suggests materials that might be useful in the drafting of these policies.

Undertaking foster carer reviews

Most obviously, each fostering service provider will have to set out how foster carer reviews are expected to be undertaken, and should cover a number of the issues set out in this guide, especially around process and expectations (see Chapter 2). For example, it will be necessary to decide whether foster carers are expected to complete FR-B2 on every occasion, or whether there is flexibility about this. Similarly, there should be clarity around the use of children's names or their initials. Practitioners and foster carers will also need to know about where the fostering panel fits with the review process. There should also be a policy in place for reviews that must be undertaken at short notice.

It may be that the service has a comprehensive policy that covers the whole range of matters that might come up within the wider requirements of undertaking a review, or alternatively some of the policies and procedures that are relevant to reviews will be covered in other policies. Whatever the preferred local style, it will be necessary to cover the following key areas.

Checks and references

Although there is no legal requirement to update any checks or references, most fostering services require DBS checks to be updated periodically; subject to registration status, fostering services can undertake this update online. Some fostering services will require an update of local authority checks and a few fostering services require annual updating of checks with children's schools and the like. This all needs to be clearly set out in policy and procedure.

Health and medicals

Similarly, many fostering services require foster carer health updates, either through the carer attending their own GP periodically, or by other methods, such as health questionnaires. The fostering service policy will need to set out where requirements such as these exist, and also consider wider aspects of promoting good health in a fostering context (see Chapter 6).

Safety and the home

There are a number of issues under this broad heading where practitioners and foster carers need to be clear about the expectations of the fostering service. This will include arrangements for the legally required annual inspection of the home, usually using a health and safety checklist as suggested by Chapman (2014), including any expectations regarding second homes or holiday homes. Most fostering services will also have specific guidance about the unannounced visit by the supervising social worker. To assist in meeting the TSDS, each fostering service will also need a policy regarding fire safety, and another setting out the issues around "safer caring". Linked to safety in the home is the issue of dogs and other pets, and this is addressed very fully by Adams (2014, forthcoming). Expectations around smoking are addressed in the relevant BAAF Practice Note (BAAF, 2007).

Skills levels and finance

Although finance is not specifically addressed within the review process, it can be a matter that creates great difficulties for fostering services and each one is required to have a policy that sets out the issues. Where payments are linked to skills levels, the fostering service will need to have written arrangements regarding the process and criteria for moving across the levels.

Employment and other paid activity

Fostering services can have different expectations about employment outside of fostering. Some consider that fostering is effectively full-time employment and have expectations that other paid work is not appropriate; other services are more flexible. This needs to be clearly set out in policy, including any stipulations in respect of child minding.

Training and development

While there are clear requirements regarding the training and development of foster carers, different fostering services will have their own detailed expectations, and policies covering this must cover approaches to achieving the TSDS, safer caring training, personal development plans, and attendance at formal training and/or support groups.

Other policies

While these are the most obvious policies that will routinely need to be considered when undertaking reviews, there will be other policies that are required either because they are stipulated in statutory guidance or National Minimum Standards, or for good practice reasons.

The following policies and procedures might well be relevant in relation to certain reviews, depending on the specific issues that have arisen during that review period (although it should be noted that this is not an exhaustive list of policies and procedures that might be relevant).

- Supervision of foster carers
- Equality and diversity
- Confidentiality
- Health of fostered children
- Managing behaviour
- Children missing from care
- Record keeping
- Education of fostered children
- Preparing for placements
- Delegated authority
- "Staying put"
- Child protection/Allegations and suspicions of harm
- Complaints
- "Whistle-blowing"

8 Conclusion

Form FR is designed for use by those fostering services committed to best practice in terms of undertaking foster carer reviews, and this guide unapologetically sets out to support those with high aspirations. It is difficult to overstate the importance of the foster carer review, and where a fostering service routinely undertakes these to a high standard, it is highly likely that this will be reflected in other areas of their practice.

Where fostering services try to take shortcuts with reviews, it is likely that other problems will be evident as opportunities are missed to address poor practice at an early stage, foster carers are allowed to neglect their training and development, and there is limited feedback from foster carers about their experience of the service. In these circumstances, it is likely that the outcomes for fostered children will be impacted upon and at worst, abuse and neglect will go undetected (see Biehal *et al*, 2014).

The largest part of this guide specifically goes through the various parts of Form FR from FR-A to FR-I, providing detailed guidance about the completion of each. This should provide supervising social workers with the information that they need to complete both their own section of the report (FR-A), and to ensure that appropriate support is made available to those responsible for the other sections.

Other chapters clarify the legal position around reviews, which it is anticipated will be helpful to many fostering practitioners, and provide a planning process for foster carer reviews – one that has been tested and implemented by fostering services to good effect. There is information about how Form FR supports the TSDS requirements, a chapter looking at the health of fostetr carers, and the penultimate chapter provides advice about the policies and procedures that fostering services will need to develop to use with Form FR.

Ultimately, the work that has gone into Form FR and this guide will only be worthwhile if it makes a helpful contribution to fostering services achieving best practice around the conduct of reviews. For this to happen, it will be necessary for fostering managers and practitioners to take up the challenge; to set high expectations and to strive to meet them.

References

Adams P (2014, forthcoming) *Dogs and Pets in Fostering and Adoption*, London: BAAF

Adams P and Dibben E (2011) *Parent and Child Fostering*, London: BAAF

BAAF (2007) *Reducing the Risks of Environmental Tobacco Smoke for Looked After Children and their Carers*, Practice Note 51, London: BAAF

Biehal N, Cusworth C and Wade J, with Clarke C (2014) *Keeping Children Safe: Allegations concerning the abuse or neglect of children in care*, London: NSPCC

Borthwick S and Lord J (2011) *Effective Fostering Panels*, London: BAAF

Chapman R (2014) *Undertaking a Fostering Assessment: A guide to collecting and analysing information for Form F (Fostering) England*, London: BAAF

Cosis Brown H (2011) *Foster Carer Reviews: Process, practicalities and best practice*, London: BAAF

Department for Education (2011a) *Fostering Services: National Minimum Standards*, London: DfE

Department for Education (2011b) *The Children Act 1989 Guidance and Regulations, Volume 4: Fostering Services*, London: DfE

Department for Education (2011c) *The Fostering Services (England) Regulations* (amended 2013), London: DfE

Hojer I, Sebba J, and Luke N (2013) *The Impact of Fostering on Foster Carers' Children: An international literature review*, Oxford: Rees Centre

Ingham M (2013) *Independent Review Mechanism Cymru Overview Report 2010–13*, London: BAAF

Lefevre M (2010) *Communicating with Children and Young People: Making a difference*, Bristol: The Policy Press

Luckock B and Lefevre M (2008) *Direct Work: Social work with children and young people in care*, London: BAAF

OFSTED (2011) *Guidance for Inspectors on our Approach to the Training, Support and Development Standards for Foster Care Issued by the Children's Workforce Development Council, No. 110038*, London: OFSTED

Pearlman D (2012) *Independent Review Mechanism (Adoption and Fostering) Annual Report 2010–11*, London BAAF, available at: www.independentreviewmechanism.org.uk/webfm_send/48

Sinclair I (2005) *Fostering Now: Messages from research*, London: Jessica Kingsley Publishers

Thomas N (2009) 'Listening to children and young people', in Schofield G and Simmonds J (eds) *The Child Placement Handbook: Research, policy and practice*, London: BAAF, pp. 63–80

UK Joint Working Party on Foster Care (1999) *UK National Standards for Foster Care*, London: NFCA